As a retired serial entre decision to dedicate my l.. lives, and preparing students for a virtuous life and career. Reading and applying the lessons learned in *Traits* is a big step in the right direction and is a must read for all sixth-grade to college-age students.

—Roy Moore

Founder and executive director of Be Strong, a nonprofit that, among many things, completed a Stand Strong Tour with Nick Vujicic, who shared an anti-bullying message with more than 1.2 million students in thirty-eight states and twenty-eight countries. Please contact *WWW.BESTRONG.GLOBAL* for more information.

For the past thirty years I have worked with preschool children as well as teenagers. I find the book Traits the most amazing character-building tool that I've ever seen!

—Kimberly Briard

Mentor coordinator, Take Stock in Children, Palm Beach County, FL

When God wanted to restore the Temple and recover its influence in shaping the culture of Israel He sent an Ezra. The same kind of commission is on Ezra G. Harvin, a modern-day Ezra who is rebuilding the Temple one life at a time!

—Dr. Lance Wallnau

Catalytic thought leader, internationally recognized speaker, business consultant, one of the premiere speakers on the subject of cultural transformation and the seven mountains, and the founder of Lance Learning Group in Dallas, Texas

I have worked to create healthy bodies and minds in children my entire adult life. My greatest desire is to encourage parents and children and then encourage them some more! Without reservations I can state that I have never read or seen anything that can build character in children like the book Traits.

—Coach Rick Andreassen

Inspirational speaker, founder of Saints International, a worldwide sports ministry for homeschooled students in the US and also with programs for orphaned children in Zambia, Guatemala, Kenya, and Haiti

I have known E. G. Harvin for over fifteen years. It's because of his integrity and overall character that I agreed to read this book.

I want everyone to know that as an educator for my entire life I have never read or seen a book that is more needed in our junior high and high school curricula. It absolutely can prepare our children for the real world in a way that is nothing short of phenomenal.

—Dr. Ed Eissey

Teacher, coach, first principal of Palm Beach Gardens High School, president of Palm Beach Community College, national board of governors, St. Jude Children's Research Hospital

This book, created for the benefit of students, was written in an easy-to-follow, common-sense manner. I plan to use it as a guide in my classes because it touches upon key and important life skills.

With deep appreciation and respect for writing such a fine, thought provoking book.

—Professor Maria Garcia

Associate professor, Palm Beach State College

I have known E. G. Harvin for many years, both as a friend and as a leader in our church.

I truly believe that this work will and should be a powerful training tool for any business. E. G. touches on good business practices through good work habits, moral habits, and fairness to the employee and employer alike.

This book is a tool that I would have used as required reading for my management team in all eleven stores I supervised.

—Paul T. Machtel

Retired vice president and store director, Jacobson's

This book, Traits, is a nice, easy read that has much impact in it.

As a principal of a large elementary public school, I see this book as a guide through all grade levels providing good things to live by! I also would believe all will benefit by reading this book.

For children, students, young adults, and those looking to rebound in life, this is a must read!

—JEFFREY A. PEGG
ELEMENTARY SCHOOL PRINCIPAL, PALM
BEACH COUNTY SCHOOLS

I have known E. G. for fifty years, and I can truly say he is a man who not only talks the talk but walks the walk.

His book is a compilation of the teachings that many of us learned in our homes, churches, and extended families in our communities. Sadly, today that is not the case. With both parents working, or with many homes managing with a single parent, the teaching of these traits is barely skimmed. It is an easy read and organized in a way that is simple to follow.

Thank you, E. G., for providing an easy-to-follow road map through the traits many of us grew up with! This is a must-have for companies as well as schools.

—BEVERLY W. CARROLL
RETIRED PRINCIPAL AND SCHOOL ADMINISTRATOR,
WAYNE COUNTY PUBLIC SCHOOLS

Ideas are powerful! They fuel the engine of creativity and production in the business world. E. G. Harvin has identified ideas that every employee needs to succeed in business and life. People are hired for skill sets and fired for their personalities. Mastering the ideas in Traits will unlock the unlimited potential in everyone.

—DALE HEDRICK

FOUNDER AND PRESIDENT, HEDRICK
BROTHERS CONSTRUCTION COMPANY

Both Donna and I have appreciated the friendship and great work of E. G. Harvin, especially this latest book, his greatest work, Traits. Not since The New England Primer, introduced in Boston in 1690 as the first textbook printed in America, has there been such a common-sense book that every American should be required to read beginning in our elementary schools and then every year of one's life. The New England Primer for a century after its introduction was the beginning textbook for students, and until well into the twentieth century it continued to be a principal text in all types of American schools: public, private, semiprivate, home, dame, parochial, etc. Today Traits is a must-read for anyone who desires success in every area of one's life. Filled with proven principles,

Traits by E. G. Harvin beautifully lays out this easy-to-read, inspiring message for us today. Thank you, E. G. Harvin.

—**KEVIN AND DONNA JESSIP**

KEVIN, GLOBAL STRATEGIC ALLIANCE PRESIDENT, AND HIS WIFE, DONNA, FAITHFULLY ADVISE AND MEET WITH GLOBAL LEADERS FREQUENTLY IN ORDER TO ADVANCE THE ORGANIZATION'S INITIATIVES FOR THE PERSECUTED CHURCH WORLDWIDE AND FOR THE PRESERVATION OF JUDEO-CHRISTIAN PRINCIPLES. KEVIN AND DONNA HAVE USED THE KNOWLEDGE GAINED IN THEIR BUSINESS CAREERS AS A CATALYST FOR FOUNDING, DEVELOPING, AND FUNDING ORGANIZATIONS DEDICATED TO IMPACTING THE WORLD FOR POSITIVE TRANSFORMATION.

*WHAT EVERY EMPLOYER
IS LOOKING FOR*

TRAITS

EZRA "E.G."
HARVIN

**CREATION
HOUSE**

TRAITS by Ezra "E. G." Harvin
Published by Creation House
A Charisma Media Company
600 Rinehart Road
Lake Mary, Florida 32746
www.charismamedia.com

Design Director: Justin Evans
Cover design by Lisa McClure

Visit the author's website: TraitsTheBook.com

Library of Congress Control Number: 2016938851
International Standard Book Number: 978-1-62998-542-8
E-book International Standard Book Number:
978-1-62998-543-5

While the author has made every effort to provide accurate telephone numbers and Internet addresses at the time of publication, neither the publisher nor the author assumes any responsibility for errors or for changes that occur after publication.

First edition

16 17 18 19 20 — 987654321

Printed in the United States of America

DEDICATION

I would first like to dedicate this book to Donna, my loving wife of forty-eight years, who passed away July 14, 2015. Her love and compassion for children was one of the contributing factors that led to the writing of this book. I would also like to dedicate the book to my daughter, Kris; my son, Dean; my daughter-in-law, Kelli; my six grandchildren, Dylan, Adam, Ashley, Austin, Alexis, and Natalie; and last but not least my great-granddaughter, Donna, who we refer to as little Donna, as she was named after my beloved wife. It's all of these people who make life worth living.

Contents

Did You Know?

Many books and Web sites are dedicated to describing the seven major centers of influence in our country and world, also known as the seven mountains of culture: the family mountain, the religious mountain, the education mountain, the media mountain, the arts and entertainment mountain, the government mountain, and the business mountain.

All young and older adults alike will have an opportunity as well as a responsibility to bring a positive influence to one or more of these seven mountains.

As you climb the mountains in your life, never forget you will be remembered far more for what you give back than for your fame and fortune.

Master the *traits* within this book, and they will take you to the top of any mountain you attempt to climb.

Preface

The wisdom in this book is not merely the invention of my own mind and experience. It is a collection of reflections and truths culled from books, Internet sources, and from professionals in their field. Some of those quoted are well-known, and others are not. However, the common thread of wisdom that runs throughout all of them makes it yet clearer that anyone seeking to gain success in any realm, or mountain, of our society must know and employ them until they are habitual to their daily life.

INTRODUCTION

Yes, it's true. Knowing the material in this book is very valuable; however, possessing the outlined traits is ultimately more valuable.

Think about it just for a moment. Isn't it logical that if you are being interviewed for a company position or you already have a position you are much more likely to obtain the position or keep the position if you are bringing value to the company that fellow interviewees or employees don't possess?

If you wish to have success and excel in a career or relationship of any kind you have no option but to master the traits outlined in this book.

Situation: You have applied for a position at a local business. Your resume was reviewed, and you have received a phone call to come in and meet Mr. Jones, the person who does all the hiring for this small but rapidly growing company. You already know, or at least should assume, that other qualified people will be applying for the same position. The questions become: Why should Mr. Jones hire you? What will you bring to the table that is superior to the other applicants?

Everything being equal, this one statement will make all the difference: "Mr. Jones, with all due respect, I can bring things to your company that cannot be taught. I am ambitious, dependable, honest, hard-working, and I have a great attitude."

These qualities and all others that you will need to make your personal and business dreams come true are in this one little book.

Note: The attributes that you promise Mr. Jones you will bring to his company must be true. They must be ingrained in you and be part of who you are. Otherwise, they may get you into a position in which you will not be able to succeed.

Have a great career, and may all your relationships, both business and personal, be real and genuine.

Have a great life! It's completely in your hands.

—Ezra "E. G." Harvin

PART 1: PERSONAL TRAITS

Integrity

Honesty

Humility

Patience

Self-Control

Correct Motives

Positive Attitude

Sense of Humor

The Personal Trait of Having

INTEGRITY

**"*I always try to do the right thing, even
when no one is watching.*"**

"Integrity is the ability to accept one's past choices and actions and act in accordance with one's" inner values.[1] Integrity is "choosing your thoughts and actions based on" personal, ingrained, honest "values rather than personal gain."[2]

It is better to be a poor man who walks with integrity than a rich man who is crooked in his ways.[3]

Always "be more concerned with your character than your reputation...Your character is who you really are, while your reputation is merely what others" believe you to be.[4]

Remember, "honesty and integrity are absolutely essential for success in...all areas of [your] life."[5] The good news is that they don't have to be learned; they are simply choices.[6] Your word must be your bond. Very simply put, "if you say you're going to do something, do it. If you start something, finish it."[7]

People with integrity "do the right thing even if no one else does, not because they think it will change the world but because they refuse to be changed by the world."[8] Knowledge is being aware of the right path to take; integrity is taking the right path.[9]

Advantages of having *integrity*:

1. You will be respected by others.

2. You will be given the benefit of the doubt.

3. You will feel good about the person you see in the mirror.

A thought to ponder: You can obtain much fame and fortune and be a failure, as success without *integrity* is failure.[10]

On a scale of one to ten, ten being perfect, I give myself a _____.

I have read, understand, and believe the points as outlined for the personal trait of having *integrity*.

_____   _____

Signature   Date

Personal Thoughts Regarding
the Trait of Having *Integrity*

Why I gave myself this point value:

What I can do to raise my point value:

Why I believe this trait is important to have in my life:

The Personal Trait of Having

HONESTY

"*I've discovered that honesty is always the best policy.*"

Someone once wisely noted that the greatest advantage of speaking the truth is that you never have to remember what you said.

In life we always have the choice of two roads: the road of honesty and the road of dishonesty. Many times the shortsighted take the road of dishonesty, while the wise take the road of honesty. The wise know the truth and value of helping others; they know that when they help others they in turn are helped.[1]

Character always overshadows wealth, and trust is a priceless asset.

"Being honest may not get you a lot of friends, but it'll always get you the right ones."[2]

In order to succeed, you will need for your customers or fellow employees to see you as reliable, dependable, credible, open, and honest.

"There are four very important words in life: *love, honesty, truth,* and *respect.*" If these are not part of your life and who you are, "you have nothing."[3]

Personal and business relationships take a lot of practice, sacrifice, pain, forgiveness, and *honesty.* Like anything of value in life, achieving good relationships will never be easy.

In a relationship *honesty* and trust are a must! If they are not present, an individual is not capable of love. So if you can't be *honest,* stay single.[4]

Advantages of having *honesty*:

1. Others will know that you are trustworthy.

2. You will be well respected.

3. You will have many true friends.

A thought to ponder: An *honest* comment never needs to be amended.

On a scale of one to ten, ten being perfect, I give myself a _____.

I have read, understand, and believe the points as outlined for the personal trait of having *honesty.*

_____   _____

Signature   Date

Personal Thoughts Regarding
the Trait of Having *Honesty*

Why I gave myself this point value:

What I can do to raise my point value:

Why I believe this trait is important to have in my life:

The Personal Trait of Having

Humility

*"I try not to think of myself more
highly than I do of others."*

True *humility* is staying teachable, regardless of how much you already know. *Humility* is the opposite of pride. Pride causes you to fail, while *humility* promotes your success. Greatness is not found in power, wealth, or position; it's discovered in character and *humility*.[1]

"Being *humble* means recognizing that we are not on Earth to see how important we can become but to see how much difference we can make in the lives of others."[2]

"True *humility* is intelligent self-respect which keeps us from thinking too highly...of ourselves." It keeps us down to Earth and reminds us how much more we can learn, even if others believe we know it all.[3] To be the greatest is an aspiration for the immature, but it is completely irrelevant to a person of *humility*.

Humility is the knowledge and "wisdom of accepting" the fact that you can "be wrong."[4]

Have "enough confidence to believe that you can solve

any...problem and enough *humility* to understand that some of your initial ideas" may be wrong. Have "enough *humility* to listen to" others who may have some good ideas of their own. *Humility* always involves being a good listener.[5]

Advantages of having *humility*:

1. You are appreciated by others.

2. You are known as a person with concern for others.

3. You are known as one who gathers all the facts before making bold statements.

A thought to ponder: *Humble* people are respected not because of what they know but because of who they are.

On a scale of one to ten, ten being perfect, I give myself a _____.

I have read, understand, and believe the points as outlined for the personal trait of having *humility*.

_____   _____

Signature   Date

Personal Thoughts Regarding the Trait of Having *Humility*

Why I gave myself this point value:

What I can do to raise my point value:

Why I believe this trait is important to have in my life:

The Personal Trait of Having

PATIENCE

"Once I realized that I wasn't perfect it became much easier to have patience with others."

"*Patience* is not the ability to wait but the ability to keep a good attitude while doing so."[1] "Two things define you: your *patience* when you have nothing and your attitude when you have everything."[2]

"*Patience* is a form of wisdom. It demonstrates that we understand and accept the fact that sometimes things must unfold in their own time."[3]

"Good things come to those who believe, [but] better things come to those who are *patient*."[4] Sometimes, no matter how much you want something to happen, all you can do is wait. Usually waiting with *patience* is the most difficult part.[5]

"Strength doesn't lie in carrying heavy loads"; a camel can do that. Strength lies in being *patient*.[6]

Being *patient* is never caused by a lack of ambition. Having *patience* simply lets others know that good things often take time to evolve.

"Showing *patience* in a moment of anger saves a thousand moments of regret."[7] When you're tempted to lose *patience* with someone, think about a time when someone has been *patient* with you.

Advantages of having *patience*:

1. Others will know that you have concern for them.

2. You are never anxious and always content.

3. It's a way of letting others know that they matter.

A thought to ponder: In order to favorably coexist with others, impatience is not an option.

On a scale of one to ten, ten being perfect, I give myself a _____.

I have read, understand, and believe the points as outlined for the personal trait of having *patience*.

_____   _____

Signature   Date

Personal Thoughts Regarding
the Trait of Having *Patience*

Why I gave myself this point value:

What I can do to raise my point value:

Why I believe this trait is important to have in my life:

The Personal Trait of Having

SELF-CONTROL

"I always say that uncontrolled emotions are juvenile."

Anyone "can criticize, complain, and condemn...but it takes character and self-control to be understanding and forgiving."[1]

A person who has *self-control* over his emotions has great power over those who don't. "*Self-control* is a key factor in achieving success. We can't control everything in life, but we can definitely control ourselves."[2]

One thing is very true: If we don't take control of our emotions, our emotions will take control of us. We cannot always "control what happens to" us, but we "can control" our "attitude toward what happens...and in that [we] will be mastering change rather than allowing it to master" us.[3] In business you will never be given an opportunity to have control of others if you can't control yourself.

Self-control is realizing that you have control over your mind and the words that come out of your mouth. Realizing this will deliver great strength, as well as an advantage in dealing with others.

If "something or someone" is "causing your blood pressure to rise, do your best to stay calm, even if you feel like throwing a fit. Acting out won't help anything... It might just put you in a bad light. And...you could end up regretting it in a big way. Remember, work on staying calm and trust that others aren't out to get you."[4]

There is no greatness without *self-control*. Development that does not include personal constraint will only guarantee mediocrity.

Advantages of having *self-control*:

1. You will always make better decisions.

2. You will have a life of contentment.

3. Your decision-making process will be
   superior to most.

A thought to ponder: The tongue is a very small muscle, but it can inflict much damage.

On a scale of one to ten, ten being perfect, I give myself a _____.

I have read, understand, and believe the points as outlined for the personal trait of having *self-control*.

_____   _____

Signature   Date

Personal Thoughts Regarding the Trait of Having *Self-Control*

Why I gave myself this point value:

What I can do to raise my point value:

Why I believe this trait is important to have in my life:

The Personal Trait of Having

CORRECT MOTIVES

"I am interested in making a lot of money so that I can help those in need."

A *correct motive* "cannot sanction a bad action."[1] Bad motives can never produce good results.

A great and noble *correct motive* is to "leave the world a better place than you found it."[2] *Correct motives* always take into account the impact that actions will have on others.

A *correct motive* for owning a company is to provide a product or service that can improve the lives of others. A *correct motive* for being an employee is to assist the owner in achieving the same goals. A *correct motive* for being in a relationship is to love and serve the one to whom you are committed.

A *correct motive* is not the end result but is always involved when the end result is good. For any goal that you may have in life, or for anything that you may wish to accomplish, you should always ask yourself the question, "Do I have *correct motives*?"

Advantages of having *correct motives*:

1. You will be trusted by others.

2. Others will know that you have their best interest in mind.

3. You will always produce results of which you can be proud.

A thought to ponder: With *correct motives* you may from time to time need to start over, but you will never fail or be considered a failure.

On a scale of one to ten, ten being perfect, I give myself a _____.

I have read, understand, and believe the points as outlined for the personal trait of having *correct motives*.

_____   _____

Signature   Date

Personal Thoughts Regarding the Trait of Having *Correct Motives*

Why I gave myself this point value:

What I can do to raise my point value:

Why I believe this trait is important to have in my life:

The Personal Trait of Having a

POSITIVE ATTITUDE

"I don't know about you, but my glass is always half full."

A *positive attitude* means thinking about achieving, believing you will achieve, and acting as if you have already achieved.[1] With a *positive attitude* come "strength, energy, motivation, and initiative."[2]

A *positive attitude* means expecting more than you should and knowing that you will accomplish more than others expect.

There may be "little difference" between two people, "but that little difference [can make] a big difference. The little difference is attitude. The big difference is whether it is positive or negative."[3]

"A negative thinker sees difficulty in every" opportunity, while a person with a *positive attitude* always "sees opportunity in" the midst of difficulties.[4] "A *positive attitude* causes a chain reaction of positive thoughts, events, and outcomes. It is a catalyst…[that] sparks extraordinary results."[5]

"If you have a *positive attitude* and...strive to give your best effort,...you will overcome [the] immediate problems and find [that] you are ready for greater challenges."[6]

The number one thing that produces a successful outcome for any project is a *positive attitude*.

Advantages of having a *positive attitude*:

1. Others will follow your lead.

2. It gives you the ability to change as needed.

3. Failure is never an option.

A thought to ponder: The difference between a great day and a bad day is attitude.[7]

On a scale of one to ten, ten being perfect, I give myself a _____.

I have read, understand, and believe the points as outlined for the personal trait of having a *positive attitude*.

_____   _____

Signature   Date

Personal Thoughts Regarding the
Trait of Having a *Positive Attitude*

Why I gave myself this point value:

What I can do to raise my point value:

Why I believe this trait is important to have in my life:

The Personal Trait of Having a

SENSE OF HUMOR

**"*I* want everyone to know that *I* love my big
noggin, because when *I'm* not using it to
think it makes a great bowling ball."**

Anyone is a lot more attractive when they have a *sense of humor.*

"Every time you are able to find some humor in a difficult situation, you win."[1] A person without a *sense of humor* is like a car without shocks—you feel every small bump in the road.[2]

"A good *sense of humor* is an escape valve for the pressures of life."[3] "Through humor you can soften some of the worst blows that life delivers, and once you find laughter, no matter how" tough or painful the situation, "you can survive."[4]

"A *sense of humor* is part of the art of leadership, of getting along with people, [and] of getting things done."[5]

A *sense of humor* "is the pole that adds balance to [our] steps as [we] walk the tightrope of life."[6] You have to have a *sense of humor* "to keep your sanity."[7]

A *sense of humor,* as with some of the other traits, needs to be controlled. You see, others are not always in a very good mood.

"If you could choose just one characteristic to get you through life, choose a *sense of humor.*"[8]

Advantages of having a *sense of humor*:

1. You are instantly more attractive.

2. People enjoy being around you.

3. People with a good *sense of humor* have a better sense of life.

A thought to ponder: You certainly can go through life without a *sense of humor,* but it will be a very long, hard road.

On a scale of one to ten, ten being perfect, I give myself a _____.

I have read, understand, and believe the points as outlined for the personal trait of having a *sense of humor.*

_____   _____

Signature   Date

Personal Thoughts Regarding the Trait of Having a *Sense of Humor*

Why I gave myself this point value:

What I can do to raise my point value:

Why I believe this trait is important to have in my life:

Part 2: Employee Traits

Hard Worker

Goal-Oriented

Ambitious

Personal Responsibility

Team Player

Self-Starter

Productive

Punctual

The Employee Trait of Being a

HARD WORKER

***"I get great reviews because I know what's
expected of me, and I do it."***

"A *hard-working* employee is one who makes the most of [his] time and who consistently produces good work."[1]

A *hard-working* employee exhibits the traits of productivity, motivation, dedication, and self-reliance.[2]

"A *hard-working* employee stays focused on the tasks before [him] and spends little time chatting with other employees....

"You will not catch a *hard-working* employee browsing the Internet for" personal information.[3] They are "ethically motivated to provide an honest day of work for [their] wages...[and take] pride in their" accomplishments.

Hard workers are motivated to do the best job they can. They "eagerly look forward to any training that might help [them] do better" and are "the first to volunteer for new projects."[4] *Hard workers* "consistently" produce work of "acceptable to excellent quality," and they look "for more work" when "everything assigned to" them is completed.

Hard workers do not require "constant supervision" and are "self-reliant and accurate."[5] They do not need "hand-holding" and are not "afraid to ask for help or additional training as needed." They are "reliable and consistently [meet] deadlines and production goals."

Hard workers are dedicated to their employers, which makes them an asset to their companies.[6]

Advantages of being a *hard worker*:

1. You are respected by your employer.

2. You may be rewarded with a higher income.

3. You will feel a great sense of accomplishment.

A thought to ponder: It is much easier to be a *hard worker* than it is to work hard at getting out of work.

On a scale of one to ten, ten being perfect, I give myself a _____.

I have read, understand, and believe the points as outlined for the employee trait of being a *hard workers*.

_____   _____

Signature   Date

Personal Thoughts Regarding the Trait of Being a *Hard Worker*

Why I gave myself this point value:

What I can do to raise my point value:

Why I believe this trait is important to have in my life:

The Personal Trait of Being

GOAL-ORIENTED

"Mr. Jones, I invited you to my office to let you know that another raise is coming your way. You have again exceeded your goal."

Theodore Roosevelt once said that when you believe you can accomplish something you are halfway there.[1]

To achieve a goal you must first define it, want it, believe it, write it down, split it up into manageable parts, review it, establish a time frame, and make it happen.

There's a difference between interests and goals. When you have an interest "in doing something you do it only when it's convenient."[2] However, when it's a true goal "you [make] no excuses" and settle for nothing but positive results.

First, determine what you want and why you want it. Once you understand what's really important your passion will get you there. Goals are accomplished by those who are consistent. They keep their eyes on the goal, as if they were wearing blinders, letting nothing distract them from achieving their objective.[3]

When you are on the bottom "keep your goal firmly in view and you will" find "renewed energy to continue the climb."[4] *Goal-oriented* people are connected with action and continue to move; "they may make mistakes, but they don't quit."[5] Every goal and "every accomplishment starts with the decision to try."[6] The only way one can fail is to stop trying.[7]

Achieving a goal is not nearly as important as the person you become by doing so.[8]

Advantages of being *goal-oriented*:

1. You are known as one who never quits.

2. You wake up every day with a purpose.

3. You know that obstacles are not the end but are simply distractions.

A thought to ponder: Whether you believe you can accomplish a goal or you believe you can't, you will always be right.[9]

On a scale of one to ten, ten being perfect, I give myself a _____.

I have read, understand, and believe the points as outlined for the employee trait of being **Goal Oriented**.

_____   _____

Signature   Date

Personal Thoughts Regarding the
Trait of Being *Goal-Oriented*

Why I gave myself this point value:

What I can do to raise my point value:

Why I believe this trait is important to have in my life:

The Personal Trait of Being

AMBITIOUS

"I can tell you, Mr. Jones, you set a great example for your fellow employees when it comes to ambition."

Ambition is wanting something you've never had and knowing that in order to obtain it you must "do something that you have never done."[1] *Ambition* is always the road to success, and hard work will be the vehicle with which to travel.[2] *Ambition* is the ability to put your fears behind you and your goals and dreams in front of you.

Ambitions are dreams—with a plan to make them a reality. Rewards are given to those who have *ambitions*. *Ambitions* take you toward the good things in life and away from the bad.

Ambition is aiming high, moving forward.[3] It's understanding that goals are not accomplished by wishful thinking but by having a plan for success. *Ambition* can overcome other things, like inexperience. Anyone with time will gain experience, but *ambition* cannot be taught.

Ambition releases our "unlimited potential."[4] Everyone has the ability to make the impossible possible. There is no one who can hold an *ambitious* person down for a long period of time. When good habits and perseverance meet with *ambition*, the end result is always victory.[5]

Advantages of being *ambitious*:

1. You're known for not needing constant supervision.

2. You cannot be easily distracted.

3. You are known for being goal-oriented.

A thought to ponder: A person's "worth is no greater than...his [or her] *ambitions*."[6]

On a scale of one to ten, ten being perfect, I give myself a _____.

I have read, understand, and believe the points as outlined for the employee trait of being *ambitious*.

_____   _____

Signature   Date

Personal Thoughts Regarding
the Trait of Being *Ambitious*

Why I gave myself this point value:

What I can do to raise my point value:

Why I believe this trait is important to have in my life:

The Employee Trait of Taking

PERSONAL RESPONSIBILITY

*"Mr. Jones, I don't have to tell you that none of us
are perfect. I do, however, want to let you know
that I really respect you for never blaming others
and always taking personal responsibility."*

Accepting *responsibility* is knowing that it's you, and you
alone, driving the car of your life. It's you, and you alone,
who determines the right and left turns in your life.[1]
"*Personal responsibility* is not only recognizing the errors
of our ways" but having the will "and ability to correct"
them.[2]

Personal responsibility is not a one-time deal but a
lifestyle. The choices we make daily ultimately shape
our lives. Once you acknowledge and take *personal
responsibility* for yourself, you are well on your way to
making the necessary changes that will transform your
life.

Circumstances such as where you were born, who your
parents are, the year of your birth, and even your gender,

are fixed. However, you can change yourself by taking *personal responsibility.*[3]

The best day of your life is the day you realize you are in complete control and that by taking *personal responsibility* you have the opportunity to become all you can be.[4] By taking *personal responsibility* you can make all of your dreams become a reality.[5]

Remember that "you are always responsible for" what you say and "how you act, no matter how you [may] feel."[6]

Advantages of taking *personal responsibility*:

1. You will feel great about your accomplishments.

2. You will be known for never blaming others.

3. Others will enjoy working with you.

A thought to ponder: No one ever brought positive change to themselves by blaming someone else.

On a scale of one to ten, ten being perfect, I give myself a _____.

I have read, understand, and believe the points as outlined for the employee trait of taking *personal responsibility.*

_____   _____

Signature   Date

Personal Thoughts Regarding the Trait of Taking *Personal Responsibility*

Why I gave myself this point value:

What I can do to raise my point value:

Why I believe this trait is important to have in my life:

The Personal Trait of Being a

TEAM PLAYER

"Mr. Jones, I have to say, you exhibit skills in working with others that I seldom see. You must have played team sports in college."

Being a *team player* is understanding that there are always views other than your own. A *team player* makes others the focal point, listens intently, praises freely, and takes the spotlight off him- or herself.[1]

Being a *team player* is one of the best contributions anyone can bring to a company. Lou Holtz, former Notre Dame football coach, said if a company is to reach its true potential, each employee must be willing to put aside his or her personal agenda for the good of the company.[2]

A *team player*, "always doing his or her best, becomes a natural leader just by example."[3] Good employees inspire themselves, while great employees inspire others and earn promotions.

In business—as Henry Ford put it—"coming together is a beginning. Keeping together is [called] progress. Working together [as a team] is [called] success."[4] Vince

Lombardi said, "The achievements" of any company "are the results of the combined effort of each individual[s]" working together toward one common goal.[5]

Working alone, we can accomplish little, but working as a team the company can be taken to the top, whereby all are rewarded.

Advantages of being a *team player:*

1. *Team players* are truly appreciated by employers.

2. They are compensated, in part, on their ability to get along with others.

3. They are held in high esteem by other employees.

A thought to ponder: Nothing secures your future like being a *team player.*

On a scale of one to ten, ten being perfect, I give myself a _____.

I have read, understand, and believe the points as outlined for the employee trait of being a *team player.*

_____   _____

Signature   Date

Personal Thoughts Regarding the Trait of Being a *Team Player*

Why I gave myself this point value:

What I can do to raise my point value:

Why I believe this trait is important to have in my life:

The Personal Trait of Being a

SELF-STARTER

"As an employee, I realize time does not stand still. Therefore, I don't stand around waiting for you to tell me it's time to go to work."

Self-starters "jumpstart new projects, wrap up unfinished business,...set and meet deadlines, [and] create and fulfill goals."[1] *Self-starters* are those who attain greatness.[2] They believe in their companies as well as themselves, and they follow their dreams. People at the top are there because they chose to be *self-starters.*

Good things come to those who obtain employment, better things come to those who work hard, and the best things come to those who work hard and are also *self-starters.*

What Coco Chanel said is true: "In order to be irreplaceable one must be different"[3]—and bring value to a company. Being a *self-starter* does just that. No one ever lost his or her job by being a *self-starter.*

A *self-starter* is the one who holds the key that drives the engine of success. "The strongest factor for success is" being a *self-starter*, believing you can accomplish what you start and "believing you deserve it."[4]

Be a *self-starter* and do your best. It might just be all you really need.

Advantages of being a *self-starter*:

1. *Self-starters* are respected and appreciated by employers.

2. They accomplish their goals in less time.

3. They are known for getting things done.

A thought to ponder: An employed person who has to constantly wait for direction will soon become unemployed, while an unemployed *self-starter* will soon become employed.

On a scale of one to ten, ten being perfect, I give myself a _____.

I have read, understand, and believe the points as outlined for the employee trait of being a *self-starter*.

_____   _____

Signature   Date

Personal Thoughts Regarding the Trait of Being a *Self-Starter*

Why I gave myself this point value:

What I can do to raise my point value:

Why I believe this trait is important to have in my life:

The Personal Trait of Being

PRODUCTIVE

"Sir, there's one thing that I know for sure. If I don't produce a profit for this company it's just a matter of time before I will be looking for a new job."

Being *productive* means to start now. When you start now instead of tomorrow you will always finish a day sooner.

I like for things to happen, and I know they will not happen on their own. That's why I'm always taking steps to make them happen.

Being *productive* is not an accident. It's when "excellence, intelligent planning, and focused effort" come together.[1] *Productive* people make "no excuses," waste no time, and have "no regrets."[2]

The goal of employment is not simply to collect a paycheck but to matter, to be *productive*, to be useful, and to make a positive difference. I realize that I am not paid for being busy but for being *productive*.

People who are *productive* are promoted. They don't ask what the company can do for them but what they can do for the company. The question is not, How can I become the best *in* the company? but, How can I become the best *for* the company?

"You must remain" *productive* and "focused on your journey to greatness."[3]

Advantages of being *productive*:

1. Goals are accomplished.

2. Promotions are obtained.

3. A *productive* person is known for not being a procrastinator.

A thought to ponder: *Productive* people start where they are, use what they have, and do what they can.

On a scale of one to ten, ten being perfect, I give myself a _____.

I have read, understand, and believe the points as outlined for the employee trait of being *productive*.

_____   _____

Signature   Date

Personal Thoughts Regarding the Trait of Being *Productive*

Why I gave myself this point value:

What I can do to raise my point value:

Why I believe this trait is important to have in my life:

The Personal Trait of Being

PUNCTUAL

"Mr. Jones, I would like for you to know that you will be recognized for punctuality at this year's employee banquet. You will receive an award for not being late for work one day within the last five years. You will also find a nice surprise in this week's paycheck."

Punctuality is a form of politeness.[1] It's a sign that you are not above others and that you appreciate the opportunity you've been given. *Punctuality* is more valuable than money. You can get more money, but you cannot get more time. "Arriving late [is] a way of saying that your own time [is] more valuable than the time of the person who [is waiting] for you."[2]

Punctuality is a choice. Employers know that *punctual* employees will make good choices in other aspects of their jobs. Successful people are *punctual*; they have order in their lives and are diligent in what they do. *Punctual* people have a determination that leads to success.

Preparedness and *punctuality* are two of the most important qualities a leader can possess.

Procrastination and *punctuality* are both habits. "Procrastination is the art of keeping up with yesterday,"[3] while *punctuality* is keeping up with today. Which one will you choose?

"Perhaps *punctuality* is...even more valuable because it is found in so few people."[4] May it be found in you.

Advantages of being *punctual*:

1. People know that you are dependable.

2. You provide a great example for others.

3. You will be judged by what you do more than by what you say.

A thought to ponder: If you wouldn't be late in picking up your paycheck, then don't be late in earning it.

On a scale of one to ten, ten being perfect, I give myself a _____.

I have read, understand, and believe the points as outlined for the employee trait of being *punctual*.

_____   _____

Signature   Date

Personal Thoughts Regarding the Trait of Being *Punctual*

Why I gave myself this point value:

What I can do to raise my point value:

Why I believe this trait is important to have in my life:

PART 3: LEADERSHIP TRAITS

Taking Ownership

Confident

Even-Tempered/Calm

Concern for Others

Leading by Example

Good Listener

Planning for Success

Persistence

The Leadership Trait of

Taking Ownership

"Good morning. I've called this meeting with the three of you so that I might commend each of you for the outstanding ways in which you have been representing this company. All three of you accept feedback gladly and never make excuses. As a result of your outstanding performances each of you will receive a bonus."

Taking ownership is accepting responsibility, being accountable, and understanding that you are in complete control of your own destiny.[1] *Taking ownership* is having a strategy, purpose, vision, and willingness to make and accept change when necessary.

People who *take ownership* understand that they must never stop learning because life is forever teaching. People who *take ownership* recognize a problem, make a plan, take action, and get results. They are confident enough to believe that they can take a company to a new level, and guess what? They can.

Always say what you mean and mean what you say, because the one who minds doesn't matter and the one who matters will appreciate it.[2]

Today is my opportunity to shape tomorrow, take control, and make positive things happen. How good tomorrow will be is determined largely by the choices I make today.

Seize the moment and make the most of it, for an entire day is made of moments.[3] People who *take ownership* "accomplish...more in a [short] period of time than" others "could ever imagine."[4]

Advantages of *taking ownership*:

1. Your boss will not be looking over your shoulder.

2. You will feel great about your accomplishments.

3. You will be trusted with important company projects.

A thought to ponder: Rather than relying on others, *taking ownership* puts you in charge of your own destiny.

On a scale of one to ten, ten being perfect, I give myself a _____.

I have read, understand, and believe the points as outlined for the leadership trait of *taking ownership*.

_____   _____

Signature   Date

Personal Thoughts Regarding the
Trait of *Taking Ownership*

Why I gave myself this point value:

What I can do to raise my point value:

Why I believe this trait is important to have in my life:

The Leadership Trait of Being

CONFIDENT

"I would like to thank each of you for taking time away from your families to attend this special, called meeting. I would like to apologize if I come across as arrogant. The fact is, I have confidence and know that I can take this company to a new level. The good news for you three is that I'm going to take you with me."

Confidence is knowing that the results will be remarkable before even one step has been taken. *Confidence* takes preparation; it's laying a solid foundation, having a plan, and having all the necessary tools to complete the project. Everything else is beyond one's control.

"What lies behind…[and] before" a person is nothing "compared to what lies" *inside* a person with *confidence*.[1] Every time a person fails he or she can gain *confidence* knowing that the world doesn't end. The fact is, we enjoy our successes, but we learn much more from our failures.[2]

Most people believe that the grass is always greener in someone else's backyard. A person with *confidence* does not buy into this myth and knows that it's all about fertilizing the grass he or she is standing on.

Everyone has limitations. When we listen to our critics their limitations become ours. When we have *confidence* we are in complete control and determine our own limitations.

Splendid things are only accomplished by those who dare to believe that they can overcome the same circumstances that the others around them face.

Advantages of being *confident*:

1. People will follow and put their trust in you.

2. Employers will provide you with additional responsibilities.

3. Others know that you are not afraid to change directions.

A thought to ponder: A person can grow only as much as his or her vision will allow.

On a scale of one to ten, ten being perfect, I give myself a _____.

I have read, understand, and believe the points as outlined for the leadership trait of being *confident*.

_____   _____

Signature   Date

Personal Thoughts Regarding
the Trait of Being *Confident*

Why I gave myself this point value:

What I can do to raise my point value:

Why I believe this trait is important to have in my life:

The Leadership Trait of Being

EVEN-TEMPERED/CALM

"I believe we all need to understand that in order to become a leader with this company or any company having a calm demeanor in difficult situations is of utmost importance."

Being *even-tempered* is having the ability to control one's emotions in the midst of a storm. Being *even-tempered* is being free from excitement. It is holding agitations within. It's maintaining tranquility and serenity in difficult situations.[1]

Even-tempered people are calm, composed, coolheaded, peaceful, serene, unruffled, and unexcitable.[2]

One of the biggest factors that hold people back from becoming good leaders is that they speak without understanding or considering what the outcome will be.

Not being calm and giving in to anger allows others to control your emotions. Aristotle noted that all people get angry from time to time; the key is that *even-tempered* people get "angry with the right person...to the right degree...at the right time...for the right purpose, and in the right way."[3]

Always be slow to anger and even slower to speak when you are angry;[4] taking words back is like trying to get toothpaste back into the tube.[5]

Advantages of being *even-tempered/calm*:

1. People enjoy working with and for you.

2. People will treat you with the respect you deserve.

3. Your *even-tempered* demeanor will be contagious.

A thought to ponder: You can never win by losing your temper.

On a scale of one to ten, ten being perfect, I give myself a _____.

I have read, understand, and believe the points as outlined for the leadership trait of being *even-tempered/ calm*.

_____   _____

Signature   Date

Personal Thoughts Regarding the Trait of Being *Even-Tempered/Calm*

Why I gave myself this point value:

What I can do to raise my point value:

Why I believe this trait is important to have in my life:

The Leadership Trait of Showing

CONCERN FOR OTHERS

"Mary, you are correct. People will only follow your lead if they know that you have their best interest at heart."

Showing *concern for others* is understanding that the only way you can become successful is to assist others in obtaining their success.

Showing *concern for others* is asking a simple question like, What can I do to help you have a better day? or, What can I do to help you with the project you are working on?

Showing *concern for others* is like making a deposit in their bank; at some future point it will come back to you with interest. No one will ever respect a person who does not first have concern for them.

One of the best ways you can show your *concern for others* is to be a good listener. It's very difficult to understand how to help someone unless they tell you where they need help. A few minutes of listening to someone will eliminate hours of guessing what their needs may be.

Never underestimate the value and impact of "a smile, a kind word," or "an honest compliment."[1] When you care more for others than they believe is necessary the results you'll receive will be far more than others will expect.

Showing *concern for others* is a sign of strength, not weakness.

Advantages of showing *concern for others*:

1. Friends will be easily obtained.

2. People will gladly follow your lead.

3. People will always be willing to do you favors.

A thought to ponder: Never be too busy to show *concern for others*.

On a scale of one to ten, ten being perfect, I give myself a _____.

I have read, understand, and believe the points as outlined for the leadership trait of showing *concern for others*.

_____   _____

Signature   Date

Personal Thoughts Regarding the Trait of Showing *Concern for Others*

Why I gave myself this point value:

What I can do to raise my point value:

Why I believe this trait is important to have in my life:

The Leadership Trait of

LEADING BY EXAMPLE

"The first thing that I want all of you to know is this:
If you are going to be leaders within this company
you need to fully understand that people are far more
impressed by what you do than what you say."

Leading by example is not putting greatness into people but getting the best out of people—because they want to give you their best.

Leading by example is having the ability to assign people to positions for which they are suited, letting them know that you believe in them, and then trusting them to do the job.

Leading by example is to walk and work beside others using the word *we* rather than *I*.

Leading by example is not just another thing that influences "others; it's the only thing."[1] More than what you say, it's what you do that impacts others.

Leading by example is empowering others to greatness. When *leading by example* you inspire others to learn more, do more, and wish to accomplish more. "If your actions inspire others to dream more, learn more, do more, and become more, you are [indeed] a leader."[2]

Albert Einstein said that *leading by "example* isn't [just] another way to teach; it's the only way."[3] A good example has much more value than good advice.[4] *Leading by example* is saying what you mean and meaning what you say.

Advantages of *leading by example*:

1. People are willing to follow your lead.

2. The people you supervise will be very productive.

3. You will be appreciated and rewarded by upper management.

A thought to ponder: People know you for what you've done, not for what you plan to do.[5]

On a scale of one to ten, ten being perfect, I give myself a _____.

I have read, understand, and believe the points as outlined for the leadership trait of *leading by example*.

Signature	Date

Personal Thoughts Regarding the Trait of *Leading by Example*

Why I gave myself this point value:

What I can do to raise my point value:

Why I believe this trait is important to have in my life:

The Leadership Trait of Being a

GOOD LISTENER

***"We all need to understand that we were given
two ears and one mouth for a reason."***

Being a *good listener* is the number one way to show that you are truly concerned for the other person's welfare.

Being a *good listener* means keeping your body still and your eyes focused on the one who is speaking.

Being a *good listener* means sitting quietly, paying attention, not interrupting, and waiting for your turn to speak. You can learn much by listening and nothing by talking. Your undivided attention has a great value to others; it also shows that they have value to you.

A great conversation is always made up of two *good listeners*. It's impossible to respond to another in a concerned way if you haven't heard a word they said.

Being a *good listener* is a way of letting others know that they, and what they have to say, matter to you. Encouraging them to talk about themselves will build respect.

A *good listener* listens with the primary intent of understanding and the secondary intent of replying.[1]

Being a *good listener* "involves hearing, sensing," interpreting, evaluating, and then responding.[2]

Advantages of being a *good listener*:

1. Others will open up to you more freely.

2. You will learn much about those around you.

3. You will understand what upper management expects of you.

A thought to ponder: "All great leaders are *good listeners*."[3]

On a scale of one to ten, ten being perfect, I give myself a _____.

I have read, understand, and believe the points as outlined for the leadership trait of being a *good listener*.

_____   _____

Signature   Date

Personal Thoughts Regarding the Trait of Being a *Good Listener*

Why I gave myself this point value:

What I can do to raise my point value:

Why I believe this trait is important to have in my life:

The Leadership Trait of

PLANNING FOR SUCCESS

"Planning for success is having a strategy that allows you to visualize the end before you start."

Planning for success is defining your objective and understanding the process. It involves teamwork and staying focused until the goal has been accomplished.

Planning for success means not allowing the circumstances of today to distract from the goals of tomorrow.

When *planning for success*, make sure that you have all necessary resources in place prior to execution.

Planning for success is knowing where you're going, how you're getting there, and when you're arriving.

Planning for success starts with a vision and ends with a job well-done.

Planning for success is the ability to break down a job into manageable parts.[1] It's not getting overwhelmed.

There are worthy goals and ambitious goals, but the goals that get accomplished faster are the ones that start with a plan for success. *Planning for success* provides a strategy that aligns with business objectives and drives improved performance.

Spending the proper time planning means you will spend less time making corrections.

Advantages of *planning for success:*

1. Others will follow your lead.

2. Accomplishing your goals will become routine.

3. You will be respected by those with whom you work.

A thought to ponder: In the words of the great Yogi Berra, "If you don't know where you're going, you'll end up someplace else."[2]

On a scale of one to ten, ten being perfect, I give myself a _____.

I have read, understand, and believe the points as outlined for the leadership trait of *planning for success.*

_____   _____

Signature   Date

Personal Thoughts Regarding the
Trait of *Planning for Success*

Why I gave myself this point value:

What I can do to raise my point value:

Why I believe this trait is important to have in my life:

The Leadership Trait of Having

PERSISTENCE

"It's vital for all of you to understand that the key to success is ambition, but what will get you to the goal line is being persistent."

Any goal worth starting is worth completing. "When you think that you can't go on, force yourself…Success is based on *persistence*, not luck."[1] *Persistence* is the key. Never stop trying, and eventually you will accomplish what others simply dream about.

Winning or accomplishing one's goal is a combination of "drive and *persistence*."[2] The desire "to make another effort or try another approach is the secret" to success.[3] Accomplishing any worthwhile goal is never easy, but it is always worth it.

"Patience, *persistence*, and" hard work are "an unbeatable" formula "for success."[4] Remember, "a river will cut through rock not because of its power but because of its *persistence*."[5]

Everyone fails, but with *persistence*, failure becomes postponed success. Victory is never far away when one has the habit of *persistence*.[6] Colin Powell wisely observed that "there are no [shortcuts or] secrets to success. It is [simply] the result of preparation, hard work, and" the *persistence* to get the job done.[7]

"Ideas are a dime a dozen. The determination [*persistence*] to see the idea through is what's priceless."[8]

Advantages of having *persistence*:

1. You'll be known as one who never gives up.

2. Others will love to follow your lead to the finish line.

3. You will often be recognized for jobs well done.

A thought to ponder: Everything in life that's worth having is worth working for.[9]

On a scale of one to ten, ten being perfect, I give myself a _____.

I have read, understand, and believe the points as outlined for the leadership trait of having *persistence*.

Signature   Date

Personal Thoughts Regarding the Trait of Having *Persistence*

Why I gave myself this point value:

What I can do to raise my point value:

Why I believe this trait is important to have in my life:

Part 4: Family Traits

Generous

Understanding Sowing

Non-Judgmental

Faithful

Trustworthy

Good Money Manager

Respect for Others

Thoughtful

The Family Trait of Being

GENEROUS

"As a family we get great satisfaction from doing things for those who can never pay us back. We believe it's a great lesson to teach our children."

Generosity is giving unselfishly to others, to those in need, and to those less fortunate. It means sharing not only financial resources but also time and talents.

We should never forget that happiness, joy, and contentment do not come from obtaining something that we don't have but in providing for others' needs.

Real *generosity* is giving when you yourself are in need, realizing that the one you give to is in greater need.

Opportunities to help the multitudes may never come, but people in need will forever be with us.[1]

Generosity is more than giving money. It's also giving your time. *Generosity* is speaking a kind word to someone who has been rude to you not because they deserve it but because it's the right thing to do.

True relationships are based on trust, honesty, and *generosity*. The greatest single quality for any family member is to show love. Yes, it's the ability to share one's love and time, and yes, that is true *generosity.*

When you see an opportunity to help, do so. You can never be *generous* "too soon...[because] you never know how soon it will be too late."[2] "We make a living by what we [earn]...but we make a life by what we give [back]."[3]

Advantages of being *generous*:

1. Others will know that you are not motivated by materialism.

2. You will have an inner peace and contented life.

3. Others will acknowledge your loving and giving ways.

A thought to ponder: A person's wealth is measured not by fame or fortune but by what they give back.

On a scale of one to ten, ten being perfect, I give myself a _____.

I have read, understand, and believe the points as outlined for the family trait of being *generous.*

_____   _____

Signature   Date

Personal Thoughts Regarding the Trait of Being *Generous*

Why I gave myself this point value:

What I can do to raise my point value:

Why I believe this trait is important to have in my life:

The Family Trait of

UNDERSTANDING SOWING

"We are a very happy family because we know that our happiness comes from giving to others. The most important thing that we understand and teach our children is to give love and respect to other family members."

Sowing and reaping is a simple concept: "What you send out comes back. What you sow, you reap. What you give, you get. What you see in others exists in you."[1]

Understanding sowing is realizing that if you do not have what you need or want, take a close look at the quality of the seeds you are sowing. Inferior seeds produce an inferior product. Sowing good seeds of love, joy, peace, patience, goodness, kindness, and generosity will generate a great harvest of loving relationships.[2]

The seeds you sow will determine if you harvest flowers or weeds. Give away at least ten percent of your earnings, and the balance will be much more enjoyable. When sowing, don't expect instant results.[3] Remember, the farmer plants in one season and harvests in a different season.

Be a giver of what you would like to receive from others. If you wish to be loved, be loving. If you wish for honesty, be honest. If you wish for respect, be respectful.

"Don't judge each day by the harvest you reap."[4] Rather, keep sowing and know that the harvest is on its way. Never be surprised if you harvest a lot more than you sow; a good harvest far exceeds that which was planted.

Advantages of *understanding sowing*:

1. People will appreciate the seeds you sow in their lives.

2. Others will in turn plant seeds in your life.

3. You will have a calm and loving family and work environment.

A thought to ponder: It's impossible to harvest a good crop without sowing good seeds.

On a scale of one to ten, ten being perfect, I give myself a _____.

I have read, understand, and believe the points as outlined for the family trait of *understanding sowing.*

_____   _____

Signature   Date

Personal Thoughts Regarding the Trait of *Understanding Sowing*

Why I gave myself this point value:

What I can do to raise my point value:

Why I believe this trait is important to have in my life:

The Family Trait of Being

Non-Judgmental

"I believe in the importance of being non-judgmental within a family, as sometimes the reason for certain behavior is unclear to us. We need to understand that there's a reason behind what everyone does or says."

We all have imperfections in our lives that could be improved. Therefore, do not judge others for their imperfections that are smaller than your own. For everyone life is a journey of becoming a better person.

Trying to understand the issues in the lives of others is far more valuable and productive than wasting time being judgmental. Never judge someone for what they look like. What's on the inside is of greater importance.

When we spend time judging others it leaves less time to judge the only one over whom we have control. To judge others is to assume that you know which road in life they are taking. When we are judgmental of others it does not define who they are but who we are.

It is always better to forgive than to judge. Life is very simple when we treat others the way we would like to be treated.

Reinhold Niebuhr was on to something when he authored what is now known as the Serenity Prayer; everyone needs to accept the things in life that cannot be changed, have the courage to change the things they can, and ask for the wisdom to know the difference.[1]

If you don't like judgmental people then don't be one.

Advantages of being *non-judgmental*:

1. People will confide in you.

2. You will have a large number of close friends.

3. You will be respected and loved by family members as well as friends.

A thought to ponder: Anyone looking for friends without faults will have no friends.

On a scale of one to ten, ten being perfect, I give myself a _____.

I have read, understand, and believe the points as outlined for the family trait of being *non-judgmental*.

_____   _____

Signature   Date

Personal Thoughts Regarding the Trait of Being *Non-Judgmental*

Why I gave myself this point value:

What I can do to raise my point value:

Why I believe this trait is important to have in my life:

The Family Trait of Being

FAITHFUL

"As a father and husband, I understand that the best example I can set for my children is to be a loving and faithful husband to their mother."

Being *faithful* is never a sacrifice, but it is always a sign of true love. There is no greater treasure than a *faithful* spouse or friend.

In marriage we say *I do*, but what it really means is *I will*—I will love you regardless, I will be truly devoted regardless, and I will be *faithful* regardless. Choosing to love, respect, and be *faithful* to only one woman are all qualities of a real man.

Being *faithful* means never having to look back and wonder what happened to your relationship or your marriage. Real men and women stay *faithful* because they don't have time to look for partners. They are too busy loving their own.

There is no such thing as being *somewhat faithful*. You are either *faithful* all the time, or you are simply unfaithful.

In any relationship *faithfulness* is never an option but always a priority.

Faithfulness is the key to inner peace, joy, and a happy and fulfilling life. *Faithfulness* is understanding that the grass is never greener and what makes grass green is fertilizing what you're standing on.

Being *faithful* extends beyond the family to all relationships, including that between an employee and an employer.

Advantages of being *faithful*:

1. People will know that you are trustworthy.

2. You have a much better chance of being in a long-lasting, loyal, and loving relationship.

3. *Faithfulness* carries over to friends, coworkers, and those in authority.

A thought to ponder: If you can't stay *faithful*, stay single, as an unfaithful spouse has little value.

On a scale of one to ten, ten being perfect, I give myself a _____.

I have read, understand, and believe the points as outlined for the family trait of being *faithful*.

_____   _____

Signature   Date

Personal Thoughts Regarding
the Trait of Being *Faithful*

Why I gave myself this point value:

What I can do to raise my point value:

Why I believe this trait is important to have in my life:

The Family Trait of Being

Trustworthy

"As a mother and especially as a wife I know that the reason we have such a great marriage is because my husband is completely trustworthy. Being trustworthy in our marriage has always been a two-way street; it applies to both of us. Everyone needs to know that you can't have love without first having trust."

Trustworthiness is priceless. Many wealthy people have left their spouses to be with poor people they could trust. *Trustworthiness* is the key that opens the door to every successful relationship.

Trust is the foundation, the essential ingredient, and the bonding glue with which all great relationships are built. Real and long-lasting marriages are not based on sex, romance, large homes, fancy cars, or big-screen TVs but are based on respect, compromise, and *trust*.

Being *trustworthy* is a trait that takes years to build and seconds to destroy—requiring a lifetime to repair.

There are "four things that you can never recover" in life: "a stone after it's thrown, a word after it's spoken,…

time after it's gone, and trust that has been lost."[1] *Trust* can be like a mirror that was broken and repaired; every time you look in it you can't help but see the cracks.

In relationships "respect is earned, honesty is appreciated, *trust* is [then] gained, [and] loyalty is returned."[2] The best compliment anyone can give you is to say, "I *trust* you." Don't ever make someone regret saying that to you.

Advantages of being *trustworthy*:

1. Others will know that your word is your bond.

2. Others will not be afraid to share personal information with you.

3. Your relationships of all kinds will be built on a strong foundation.

A thought to ponder: *Trustworthiness* is the foundation of telling someone that you are going to do something and then doing it.

On a scale of one to ten, ten being perfect, I give myself a _____.

I have read, understand, and believe the points as outlined for the family trait of being *trustworthy*.

_____   _____
Signature   Date

Personal Thoughts Regarding the Trait of Being *Trustworthy*

Why I gave myself this point value:

What I can do to raise my point value:

Why I believe this trait is important to have in my life:

The Family Trait of Being a

GOOD MONEY MANAGER

*"As a father and husband not only do I have
to be a hard worker in order to support and
provide for my family, but we have to set money
aside each and every week to make sure that
our future will be as bright as our present."*

Being a *good money manager* starts by not spending money
that you don't have on things you don't need. The key to a
successful life is simply this: When you stop buying items
you don't need, you have more time and money to enjoy
the real things that matter—and that's each other.

Good money management is very simple. Either you
control it, or it controls you. Nearly half of Americans
would have trouble finding four hundred dollars to pay
for an emergency.[1] If you don't have a plan for moving
forward, in all likelihood you will move backward.

Money is only a means to an end; your reason for
making money should always be of greater value than the
money itself. Ultimately, it's not what you earn that will
determine your success but what you save.

All money you save goes toward making your future more secure. All money you spend on things you don't need goes toward securing someone else's future.

Living a contented and stress-free life is knowing that you are well prepared for rainy days and at the same time are making a difference. Helping others is one of the best investments you will ever make.

Be sure of why you're working, because success is just the beginning. The real value, happiness, lies in enjoying what you have.

Advantages of being a *good money manager*:

1. There will be little financial stress in your life.

2. You will have great credit scores.

3. You will have funds to take advantage of good investment opportunities.

A thought to ponder: If you would be embarrassed for others to review your bank statement, then you may need to work on your money management.

On a scale of one to ten, ten being perfect, I give myself a _____.

I have read, understand, and believe the points as outlined for the family trait of being a *good money manager*.

_____   _____

Signature   Date

Personal Thoughts Regarding the Trait of Being a *Good Money Manager*

Why I gave myself this point value:

What I can do to raise my point value:

Why I believe this trait is important to have in my life:

The Family Trait of Showing

RESPECT FOR OTHERS

*"As husband and wife we have a tremendous
respect for each other. We understand that being
a good person does not depend on religion, status
in life, race, or skin color. Good and decent
people always treat others with respect."*

Respecting others starts with *respecting* yourself. You can never give away something that you don't have. *Respect others* even if they don't respect you, and never allow anyone to determine how you feel about yourself.

Respect is a very simple concept. It's treating others the way you would want them to treat you. This one little reality, if practiced by all, would completely eliminate bullying in schools and families as well as the workplace. Never underestimate the power of *respecting others. Respecting* someone costs nothing but will add great value to them. Even a smile may allow someone to have a brighter day.

It is not important that you like or dislike a person, but it is important that you *respect* each one as a human being. People are different; no two people have the same life experiences. No two people share the same realities of life, but everyone needs to continue to learn and to be respected. *Respect* the wrong, the weak, and the elderly— because at some point you will be all three.

You don't need to know someone well in order to show *respect*. Remember that everyone is fighting their own battles and understand that though we are all different, that difference is not good or bad; it is simply different. You need to understand that a large percent of all human desires are the same as yours. Never disrespect a person because of the 5 percent that makes him or her different.

Respecting others is a form of sowing; it's giving what you would like to receive. Love, honesty, and *respect* are all things that everyone would like to receive. Give, and you get in return.

Advantages of showing *respect for others*:

1. People will *respect* you.

2. Others will admire and confide in you.

3. Others will give you the benefit of the doubt.

A thought to ponder: *Respect* cannot be demanded but is given to those who deserve it.

On a scale of one to ten, ten being perfect, I give myself a _____.

I have read, understand, and believe the points as outlined for the family trait of showing *respect for others*.

_____   _____
Signature   Date

Personal Thoughts Regarding the Trait of Showing *Respect for Others*

Why I gave myself this point value:

What I can do to raise my point value:

Why I believe this trait is important to have in my life:

The Family Trait of Being

THOUGHTFUL

"We both fully understand that being thoughtful costs very little and sometimes nothing. It's simply understanding the little things in life that mean so much to the person you love. My wife doesn't desire expensive gifts, but she does love a tender shoulder massage. As for me, I enjoy fishing, and my wife enjoys me having the pleasure when I can."

Thoughtfulness is a great way to show that love is not just a word but an action.

If you have an opportunity to be *thoughtful* and don't follow through it's like wrapping a present and leaving it in the closet. There is never a gift too small to give when wrapped in love with a bow of *thoughtfulness* on top.

Showing *thoughtfulness* sends a message of love directly to someone's heart. The most romantic and loving gifts always come from the heart, not the wallet. Giving of your time can be a great gift of *thoughtfulness*. Strong and lasting relationships are always made up of *thoughtful* gifts along the way.

People who wish to show concern can use words. People who really care let their actions do the talking.

Being *thoughtful* is seeing through the eyes of others, hearing through the ears of others, and feeling through the hearts of others.[1]

Advantages of being *thoughtful*:

1. You will have strong, loving relationships.

2. Your home will be a place of peace and calmness.

3. You will be rewarded and honored with love and respect.

A thought to ponder: Being *thoughtful* is a great way of showing love and concern for others.

On a scale of one to ten, ten being perfect, I give myself a _____.

I have read, understand, and believe the points as outlined for the family trait of being *thoughtful*.

_____   _____
Signature   Date

Personal Thoughts Regarding the Trait of Being *Thoughtful*

Why I gave myself this point value:

What I can do to raise my point value:

Why I believe this trait is important to have in my life:

Epilogue

If the material within the pages of this one little book is retained and put into practice—even in part—it will always enable people to be better and more productive.

The material, although primarily designed to benefit employees, and thus companies, also holds true for any business or personal relationship.

Two Thoughts to Ponder:

1. What subject taught in our high schools today provides more assistance, more value, to our young people than these thirty-two traits?

2. What company would not be thrilled to interview a young man or woman that brought this book, with all traits signed, to an interview?

Journal

Notes

Part 1: Personal Traits

Integrity

1. Lynne Namka, quoted at http://www.betterworld. net/quotes/integrity-quotes.htm (accessed March 2, 2016).

2. Zig Ziglar, Twitter post, February 22, 2015, 8:04 p.m., http://twitter.com/thezigziglar.

3. Proverbs 28:6, author's paraphrase.

4. John Wooden, quoted at http://www.brainyquote. com/quotes/quotes/j/johnwooden163015.html (accessed March 16, 2016).

5. Zig Ziglar, Facebook post, February 27, 2014, https://www.facebook.com/ZigZiglar/.

6. Ibid.

7. Epictetus, quoted at http://www.azquotes.com/ quote/767772 (accessed March 2, 2016).

8. Michael Josephson, quoted at http:// whatwillmatter.com/2012/10/quote-people-of-character-do-the-right-thing-even-if-no-one-else-does-not-because-they-think-it-will-change-the-world-but-because-they-refuse-to-be-changed-by-the-world-michael-josephson/ (accessed March 2, 2016).

9. M. H. McKee, quoted at http://www.goodreads. com/quotes/610970-wisdom-is-knowing-the-right-path-to-take-integrity-is (accessed March 2, 2016).

10. Unknown author.

Honesty

1. Napoleon Hill, quoted at http://napoleonhill. wwwhubs.com/ (accessed March 22, 2016).

2. John Lennon, quoted at http://www.goodreads. com/quotes/641429-being-honest-may-not-get-you-a-lot-of-friends (accessed April 4, 2016).

4. Unknown author.

5. Unknown author.

Humility

1. William Arthur Ward, quoted at http:// likesuccess.com/topics/23150/prestige (accessed April 30, 2016).

2. Gordon B. Hinckley, quoted at http://www. goodreads.com/quotes/70882-being-humble-means-recognizing-that-we-are-not-on-earth (accessed April 30, 2016).

3. Ralph W. Sockman, quoted at http://www. brainyquote.com/quotes/quotes/r/ralphwsoc125770.html (accessed April 22, 2016.)

4. Richard Paul Evans and Michael Vey, quoted at http://www.eaglelaunch.com/wise-humility/ (accessed July 6, 2016).

5. Larry Tesler, quoted in Dan Saffer, *Designing for Interaction* (San Francisco, CA: New Riders, 2006).

Patience

1. Joyce Meyer, Battlefield of the Mind: Winning the Battle in Your Mind (Brentwood, TN: Warner Faith, 2002).

2. While this quote is often attributed to an anonymous speaker, this statement is also frequently attributed to Imam Ali. See http://thedailyquotes.com/two-things-define-you-4/ (accessed April 22, 2016).

3. Jon Kabat-Zinn, Full Catastrophe Living (New York, NY: Random House, 2013).

4. Unknown, see http://thedailyquotes.com/

good-things-come-to-those-who-believe/ (accessed March 17, 2016).

5. Unknown, see http://www.thequotepedia.com/ sometimes-no-matter-how-much-you-want-for-things-to-happen-all-you-can-do-is-wait-and-usually-waiting-is-the-hardest-part/ (accessed March 17, 2016).

6. Imam Ali, quoted at http://justaliquotes.blogspot. com/2014/09/strength-doesnt-lie-in-carrying-heavy.html (accessed March 25, 2016).

7. Imam Ali, quoted at http://www.thequotepedia. com/a-moment-of-patience-in-a-moment-of-anger-saves-a-thousand-moments-of-regret-patience-quotes/ (accessed April 4, 2016).

Self-Control

1. Dale Carnegie, quoted at http://www.goodreads. com/quotes/20907-any-fool-can-criticize-complain-and-condemn-and-most-fools-do (accessed June 21, 2016).

2. Jan Mckingley Hilado, quoted at http://www. goodreads.com/quotes/740187-self-control-is-a-key-factor-in-achieving-success-we-can-t (accessed May 9, 2016.)

3. Brian Tracy, http://www.brainyquote.com/quotes/ quotes/b/briantracy125679.html (accessed April 30, 2016).

4. Unknown author.

Correct Motives

1. W. M. L. Jay, quoted at http://quotesgram.com/ quotes-about-bad-motives/ (accessed February 28, 2016).

2. Patricia Cornwell, quoted at http://www. goodreads.com/quotes/66631-do-no-harm-and-leave-the-world-a-better-place (accessed April 4, 2016).

Positive Attitude

[1] Remez Sasson, quoted at http://www.successconsciousness.com/index_000033.htm (accessed June 16, 2016).

[2] Ibid.

[3] W. Clement Stone, quoted at http://www.brainyquote.com/quotes/quotes/w/wclements193770.html (accessed May 14, 2016).

[4] Winston Churchill, quoted at http://www.self-help-and-self-development.com/positive_thinking_quotes.html (accessed May 31, 2016).

[5] Wade Boggs, quoted at http://www.brainyquote.com/quotes/quotes/w/wadeboggs311616.html (accessed May 31, 2016).

[6] Pat Riley, quoted at http://www.brainyquote.com/quotes/quotes/p/patriley147924.html (accessed March 26, 2016).

[7] Dennis S. Brown, quoted at http://www.bestsayingsquotes.com/quote/the-only-difference-between-a-good-day-and-a-bad-day-207.html (accessed February 26, 2016).

Sense of Humor

[1] Unknown author.

[2] Based on Henry Ward Beecher's quote, "A person without a sense of humor is like a wagon without springs. It's jolted by every pebble on the road." Quoted at http://www.brainyquote.com/quotes/quotes/h/henrywardb161732.html (accessed May 22, 2016).

[3] Richard G. Scott, quoted at https://www.lds.org/general-conference/2012/04/how-to-obtain-revelation-and-inspiration-for-your-personal-life?lang=eng&_r=1 (accessed June 15, 2016).

4. Bill Cosby, quoted at http://www.brainyquote. com/quotes/quotes/b/billcosby401323.html (accessed June 17, 2016).

5. Dwight D. Eisenhower, quoted at http://www.goodreads.com/ quotes/36270-a-sense-of-humor-is-part-of-the-art-of.

6. William Arthur Ward, quoted at http://www. brainyquote.com/quotes/quotes/w/williamart131334.html (accessed May 15, 2016).

7. Lance Bass, quoted at http://www.brainyquote. com/quotes/quotes/l/lancebass195496.html (accessed April 30, 2016).

8. Jennifer Jones, quoted at http://www.brainyquote. com/quotes/quotes/j/jenniferjo131326.html (accessed March 15, 2016).

Part 2: Employee Traits

Hard Worker

1. Betsy Gallup, "Brief Description of a Hard-Working Employee," *The Nest*, http://woman.thenest. com/brief-description-hardworking-employee-5098.html (accessed May 14, 2016).

2. Ibid.

3. Ibid.

4. Ibid.

5. Ibid.

6. Ibid.

Goal-Oriented

1. Theodore Roosevelt, quoted at http://www. brainyquote.com/quotes/quotes/t/theodorero380703.html (accessed April 16, 2016).

2. Kenneth Blanchard, quoted at http://www.
goodreads.com/quotes/73713-there-s-a-difference-between-
interest-and-commitment-when-you-re-interested (accessed
May 25, 2016).

3. Lou Holz, quoted at http://likesuccess.com/
topics/9420/blinders (accessed May 25, 2016).

4. Denis Waitley, quoted at http://www.ranker.
com/list/a-list-of-famous-denis-waitley-quotes/reference
(accessed June 11, 2016).

5. Conrad Hilton, quoted at http://www.brightquotes.
com/fai_fr.html (accessed March 31, 2016).

6. Unknown author.

7. Chris Bradford, quoted at http://www.forbes.com/
sites/ekaterinawalter/2013/12/30/30-powerful-quotes-on-
failure/#1b04bbeb15d3 (accessed March 31, 2016).

8. Zig Ziglar, quoted at http://www.brainyquote.com/
quotes/quotes/z/zigziglar120890.html (accessed June 5, 2016).

9. Henry Ford, quoted at https://www.goodreads.
com/author/quotes/203714.Henry_Ford (accessed June 5,
2016).

Ambitious

1. Thomas Jefferson, quoted at https://www.
monticello.org/site/research-and-collections/if-you-want-
something-you-have-never-had-quotation (accessed June 6,
2016).

2. Bill Bradley, quoted at http://www.brainyquote.
com/quotes/quotes/b/billbradle384430.html (accessed June
6, 2016).

4. Donald J. Trump, quoted at http://www.goodreads.
com/quotes/45247-get-going-move-forward-aim-high-plan-
a-takeoff-don-t (accessed May 30, 2016).

5. Elle Sommer, quoted at http://livepurposefullynow.

com/release-your-unlimited-potential/ (accessed March 17, 2016).

6. Herbert Kaufman, quoted at http://www.azquotes.com/quotes/topics/persistence.html (accessed June 17, 2016).

7. Marcus Aurelius, quoted at http://www.goodreads.com/quotes/120683-a-man-s-worth-is-no-greater-than-the-worth-of (accessed April 23, 2016).

Personal Responsibility

1. Les Brown, quoted at http://www.brainyquote.com/quotes/quotes/l/lesbrown387329.html (accessed June 28, 2016).

2. Yehuda Berg, quoted at http://www.brainyquote.com/quotes/quotes/y/yehudaberg536660.html (accessed June 18, 2016).

3. Jim Rohn, quoted at http://www.azquotes.com/quote/249560 (accessed June 4, 2016).

4. Bob Moawad, quoted at http://www.goodreads.com/quotes/30579-the-best-day-of-your-life-is-the-one-on (accessed June 4, 2016).

5. Les Brown, quoted at https://www.goodreads.com/author/quotes/57803.Les_Brown (accessed June 4, 2016).

6. Robert Tew, quoted at http://thoughtcatalog.com/jamie-kensinger/2016/03/17-quotes-that-will-inspire-you-to-take-responsibility-for-your-decisions/ (accessed June 4, 2016).

Team Player

1. Katzenbach and Smith, quoted at http://heartquotes.com/teamwork-quotes.html (accessed March 20, 2016).

2. Lou Holtz, quoted at http://heartquotes.com/teamwork-quotes.html (accessed March 20, 2016).

3. Joe DiMaggio, quoted at http://www.notable-quotes.com/d/dimaggio_joe.html (accessed June 18, 2016).

4. Henry Ford, quoted at http://www.forbes.com/sites/erikaandersen/2013/05/31/21-quotes-from-henry-ford-on-business-leadership-and-life/#2254edc23700 (accessed March 20, 2016).

5. Vince Lombardi, quoted at http://heartquotes.com/teamwork-quotes.html (accessed March 20, 2016).

Self-Starter

1. Jeff Davidson, *The 60 Second Self-Starter* (Avon, MA: Adams Business, 2008).

2. Napoleon Hill and W. Clement Stone, *Success Through a Positive Mental Attitude* (New York, NY: Pocket Books, 1977), 107.

3. Coco Chanel, quoted at http://www.brainyquote.com/quotes/quotes/c/cocochanel382612.html (May 31, 2016).

4. Unknown author, quote available at http://tipsinterviews.blogspot.com/2013/12/quotes-for-success.html (May 31, 2016).

Productive

1. Paul J. Meyer, quoted at http://launchyourgenius.com/2014/10/27/inspiring-quotes-productivity/ (accessed May 5, 2016).

2. Dr. Steve Maraboli, quoted at http://www.goodreads.com/quotes/tag/no-regrets (accessed May 5, 2016).

3. Les Brown, quoted at http://www.brainyquote.com/quotes/quotes/l/lesbrown379155.html (accessed May 17, 2016).

Punctual

[1.] Louis XVIII is said to have stated, "Punctuality is the politeness of kings." See http://www.budbilanich.com/punctuality-the-politeness-of-kings-and-a-key-to-positive-personal-impact/ (accessed June 18, 2016).

[2.] Karen Joy Fowler, quoted at http://www.goodreads.com/quotes/tag/punctuality (accessed June 30, 2016).

[3.] Don Marquis, quoted at http://www.brainyquote.com/quotes/quotes/d/donmarquis107414.html (accessed June 7, 2016).

[4.] Sterling W. Sill, quoted at http://www.picturequotes.com/perhaps-punctuality-is-a-quality-made-even-more-valuable-because-it-is-found-in-so-few-people-quote-264376 (accessed May 25, 2016).

Part 3: Leadership Traits

Taking Ownership

[1.] Unknown author, quoted at https://www.askideas.com/71-responsibility-quotes-and-sayings/ (accessed May 17, 2016).

[2.] Based on Dr. Seuss's famous statement, "Be who you are and say what you feel because those who mind don't matter and those who matter don't mind." Quoted at http://www.quotationspage.com/quotes/Dr._Seuss (accessed March 22, 2016).

[3.] Paul Coelho, quoted at http://www.picturequotes.com/the-day-is-made-up-of-24-hours-and-an-infinite-number-of-moments-we-need-to-be-aware-of-those-quote-442669 (accessed June 30, 2016).

[4.] Brian Tracy, quoted at http://onstrategyhq.com/

resources/define-your-goals-accomplish-more/ (accessed June 30, 2016).

Confident

1. Ralph Waldo Emerson, quoted at http://www.goodreads.com/quotes/15579-what-lies-behind-us-and-what-lies-before-us-are (accessed June 30, 2016).

2. Samuel Smiles, quoted at http://www.goodreads.com/quotes/390439-we-learn-wisdom-from-failure-much-more-than-from-success (accessed March 16, 2016).

Even-Tempered/Calm

1. See http://www.wisdomcommons.org/virtue/116-serenity/quotes (accessed March 12, 2016).

2. *Collins Thesaurus of the English Language—Complete and Unabridged 2nd edition* (New York, NY: HarperCollins, 2002), s.v. "even-tempered."

3. Aristotle, quoted at http://www.brainyquote.com/quotes/quotes/a/aristotle132211.html (accessed March 17, 2016).

4. See James 1:19.

5. Lebron James, quoted at http://www.azquotes.com/quote/1386190 (accessed March 17, 2016).

Concern for Others

1. Leo Buscaglia, quoted at http://www.quotesvalley.com/quotes/power/page/23/ (accessed March 26, 2016).

Leading by Example

1. Albert Schweitzer, quoted at https://www.entrepreneur.com/article/243861 (accessed February 27, 2016).

2. John Quincy Adams, quoted at http://www.

northbaybusinessjournal.com/csp/mediapool/sites/NBBJ/
IndustryNews/story.csp?cid=4180440&sid=778&fid=181
(accessed March 5, 2016).

3. Albert Einstein, quoted at http://thinkexist.com/
quotation/example_isn-t_another_way_to_teach-it_is_the_
only/327436.html (accessed March 17, 2016).

4. Unknown author.

5. Unknown author.

Good Listener

1. Steven R. Covey, *The 7 Habits of Highly Effective People* (New York, NY: Simon & Schuster, 2013).

2. William L. Maw, *The Work–Life Equation* (Santa Barbara, CA: Praeger, 2015), 55.

3. Ryan Alan Smith, *Lessons at 6:00 AM* (Bloomington, IN: WestBow Press, 2016).

Planning for Success

1. Erik Fisher, quoted at http://www.huffingtonpost.com/peter-banerjea/beating-procrastination-7_b_9036142.html (accessed April 27, 2016).

2. Yogi Berra, quoted at https://www.goodreads.com/author/quotes/79014.Yogi_Berra (accessed March 5, 2016).

Persistence

1. Unknown author, quoted at http://www.fueldabook.com/fuelisms/when-you-think-you-cant-go-on-force-yourself-to-keep-going-your-success-is-based-on-persistence-not-luck-3 (accessed May 30, 2016).

2. Denis Waitley, quoted at http://www.brainyquote.com/quotes/quotes/d/deniswaitl146916.html (accessed May 16, 2016).

3. Ibid.

4. Napoleon Hill, quoted at http://www.quotesvalley.com/patience-persistence-and-perspiration-make-an-unbeatable-combination-for-success-7/ (accessed April 20, 2016).

5. Jim Watkins, quoted at http://www.jameswatkins.com/articles-2/hopeful/quotes/ (accessed June 30, 2016).

6. See Herbert Kaufman, http://www.forbes.com/quotes/4309/ (accessed June 30, 2016).

7. Colin Powell, quoted at http://www.gge.co.jp/newsarticle/there-is-no-shortcut-to-success/ (accessed June 12, 2016).

8. Robert Dieffenbach, quoted at http://www.goodreads.com/quotes/807790-million-dollar-ideas-are-a-dime-a-dozen-the-determination (accessed March 31, 2016).

9. Theodore Roosevelt said, "Nothing in the world is worth having or worth doing unless it means effort, pain, difficulty." Quoted at http://www.goodreads.com/quotes/312751-nothing-in-the-world-is-worth-having-or-worth-doing (accessed April 20, 2014).

Part 4: Family Traits

Generous

1. See Matthew 26:11.

2. Ralph Waldo Emerson, quoted at http://www.brainyquote.com/quotes/quotes/r/ralphwaldo106295.html (accessed May 30, 2016).

3. Winston Churchill, quoted at http://www.brainyquote.com/quotes/quotes/w/winstonchu131192.html (accessed February 10, 2016).

Understanding Sowing

[1] Zig Ziglar, quoted at http://www. dailyinspirationalquotes.in/2015/10/24/life-is-an-echo-what-you-send-out-comes-back-what-you-sow-you-reap-what-you-give-you-get-what-you-see-in-others-exists-in-you-zig-ziglar/ (accessed March 18, 2016).

[2] See Galatians 5:22.

[3] See Karen Schmidt, "Grow better leaders by following the laws of reaping and sowing," *HR Daily Community,* August 26, 2014, http://community.hrdaily.com.au/profiles/blogs/grow-better-leaders-by-following-the-laws-of-reaping-and-sowing (accessed June 30, 2016).

[4] Robert Louis Stevenson, quoted at http://www.brainyquote.com/quotes/quotes/r/robertloui101230.html (accessed June 6, 2016).

Non-Judgmental

[1] Reinhold Niebuhr's Serenity Prayer may be found at http://www.beliefnet.com/prayers/protestant/addiction/serenity-prayer.aspx (accessed February 10, 2016).

Trustworthy

[1] Unknown author.

[2] Auliq Ice, quoted at http://www.goodreads.com/quotes/7079536-respect-is-earned-honesty-is-appreciated-trust-is-gained-loyalty (accessed June 30, 2016).

Good Money Manager

[1] See Neal Gabler, "The Secret Shame of Middle-Class Americans," *The Atlantic,* May 2016, www.theatlantic.com/magazine/archive/2016/05/my-secret.../476415/ (accessed July 29, 2016).

Thoughtful

1. Alfred Adler, quoted at http://www.goodreads. com/quotes/776552-seeing-with-the-eyes-of-another-listening-with-the-ears/ (accessed June 30, 2016).

TRAITS: THE POSTER

The poster, measuring two feet wide by three feet long, is designed for both classrooms and businesses.

The poster is designed not only to be a constant reminder for students as well as employees but also to make a powerful statement to customers.

For more information and to purchase both books and posters please visit www.traitsthebook.com

About the Author

Ezra "E. G." Harvin has been a business owner for more than forty years. He has dealt with hundreds of employees in both his own companies as well as those of his friends. E. G. is now president and CEO of the Insurance Associates of the Palm Beaches, Inc. He is well qualified when it comes to knowing what traits are missing in the lives of employees.

E. G.'s passion for children prompted him to write this book. He feels strongly that our junior high and high schools across the country could and should be doing more, not only in preparing our children for the workplace but for life in general.

E. G. was born in North Carolina, where he grew up on a farm as the youngest of five children. He moved to Connecticut at the age of nineteen, where he met Donna, his wife since 1967. He has one daughter, one son, six grandchildren, and one great-granddaughter. E. G. and Donna have resided in West Palm Beach, Florida, since 1995. E. G., in his spare time, works with two different nonprofit organizations, both of which are fully committed to improving the lives of our young people.

Contact the Author

Visit the author's Web site at TraitsTheBook.com.

Ezra "E. G." Harvin may be reached by e-mail at TraitsTheBook@gmail.com. Contact him by phone at 1 (800) 680-0000 or by mail at:

> Traits the Book, LLC
> 4521 PGA Blvd.
> PMB 410
> Palm Beach Gardens, FL 33418